My name is

Ella Annice Kuzjak

I was baptized on

My godparents are

Grandparents, Dee and Papu

(*John Daniel Little*)
(*Carol Ann Little*)

I first came to the table of the Lord

at

St. Thomas Aquinas Church

on

Saturday, May 10, 2014

My First Holy Communion: Prayers for a Lifetime

2013 Fourth Printing This Edition
2011 Third Printing This Edition
2010 First and Second Printing This Edition

Written and compiled by Sophie Piper
Illustrations copyright © 2010 Angelo Ruta
This edition copyright © 2010 Lion Hudson

The moral rights of the author and illustrator
have been asserted

Originally published by:
Lion Hudson plc
Wilkinson House, Jordan Hill Road,
Oxford OX2 8DR, England
www.lionhudson.com

Published in the United States and Canada
by Paraclete Press, 2010.

ISBN 978-1-55725-696-6

10 9 8 7 6 5 4

Acknowledgments
All unattributed prayers are by Sophie Piper
and Lois Rock, copyright © Lion Hudson.
The prayers by Victoria Tebbs (on pages 45 and
60) are copyright © Lion Hudson.
Bible extracts are taken or adapted from
the *Good News Bible*, published by The Bible
Societies/HarperCollins Publishers Ltd, UK ©
American Bible Society 1966, 1971, 1976, 1992,
used by permission.
The Lord's Prayer (page 34) is extracted from
The Book of Common Prayer, the rights of which
are vested in the Crown in perpetuity within
the United Kingdom, and is reproduced by
permission of Cambridge University Press, Her
Majesty's Printers.

Typeset in 14/18 Throhand Regular
Printed and bound in China by Printplus Ltd

My First
Holy Communion
PRAYERS FOR A LIFETIME

Sophie Piper ✤ *Angelo Ruta*

Paraclete Press
Brewster, Massachusetts

Contents

The God Who Made Me

Thank you, great Maker God,
that in your great wide world
you made a space for me.

Thank you, great Maker God,
that I am as I am –
a part of your wide world.

Praise the Lord

Praise the Lord from heaven,
all beings of the height!
Praise him, holy angels
and golden sun so bright.

Praise him, silver moonlight,
praise him, every star!
Let your praises shine
throughout the universe so far.

Praise the Lord from earth below,
all beings of the deep!
Lightning, flash! You thunder, roar!
You ocean creatures, leap.

Praise him, hill and mountain!
Praise him, seed and tree.
Praise him, all you creatures
that run the wide world free.

Let the mighty praise him.
Let the children sing.
Men and women, young and old:
Praise your God and king.

From Psalm 148

The Lord God made them all

All things bright and beautiful,
All creatures great and small,
All things wise and wonderful,
The Lord God made them all.

Cecil Frances Alexander (1818–95)

The little bugs that scurry,
The little beasts that creep
Among the grasses and the weeds
And where the leaves are deep:
All of them were made by God
As part of God's design.
Remember that the world is theirs,
Not only yours and mine.

Glory to God

Thank you, God,
for the unchanging
patterns of the seasons:
the frosts of winter
melting into moist spring,
the rain-soaked buds
unfolding into bright summer,
the flowers fading and falling
in the autumn mist
leaving the year cold and bare,
lit by a pale sun
and the golden promise
of your unfailing love.

Glory be to the Father, and to the Son, and to the Holy Spirit. As it was in the beginning, is now, and ever shall be, world without end. Amen.

I Am God's Child

O God,

When Jesus was baptized,
you declared him your Son
and strengthened him with your Holy Spirit.

I too was baptized.
Help me to live as your child
and strengthen me with your Holy Spirit.

God's kingdom

Jesus called the children to him and said,
"Let the children come to me and do not stop them,
because the kingdom of God belongs to such as these."

Luke 18:16

The kingdom of God
is like a tree
growing through all eternity.

In its branches, birds may nest;
in its shade, we all may rest.

Each new day

God has baptized the day
in the dark waters of night;
now it rises clean and shining,
bright with the gold light of heaven.

May I step bravely into this day
determined to walk the way of goodness
as God's own child
under God's own heaven.

Lord Jesus,
Make me as kind to others
as I would want to be to you.

Make me as generous to others
as I would want to be to you.

May I take time to help them
as I would want to take time to help you.

May I look into the faces of those I meet
and see your face.

Based on Matthew 25:37–40

God cares for me

God feeds the birds that sing from the treetops;
God feeds the birds that wade by the sea;
God feeds the birds that dart through the meadows;
So will God take care of me?

God clothes the flowers that bloom on the hillside;
God clothes the blossom that hangs from the tree;
As God cares so much for the birds and the flowers
I know God will take care of me.

A prayer based on Jesus' Sermon on the Mount,
Matthew 6

Loved and Forgiven

Take my wrongdoing
and throw it away,
down in the deep of the sea;
welcome me into your kingdom of love
for all of eternity.

Based on Micah 7:18–20

25

Seeing myself clearly

Dear God,
For the silly things I have done wrong
I am sorry.

For the serious things I have done wrong
I am sorry.

For the things I didn't even know
   were wrong
I am sorry.

For all the things I need to put right
Make me strong.

Dear God,
I am your lost sheep.
Please find me.
Please take me home.

Being honest

Dear God,
Please forgive me for saying sorry when I wasn't. Please
forgive me for not feeling sorry even now. Please help me
untangle my muddled feelings.

Dear God,
I am not yet ready to say sorry for what I did
because I am still trying to pretend that I did not
do it.

Please help me to be honest with myself so I can
be honest with others.

God, have mercy on me, a sinner!

From Jesus' parable of the Pharisee and the tax collector, Luke 18:13

Forgiveness

I told God everything:
I told God about all the wrong things I had done.
I gave up trying to pretend.
I gave up trying to hide.
I knew that the only thing to do was to confess.

And God forgave me.

Based on Psalm 32:5

O God,
I have done so many things wrong.
I am surrounded by dark clouds of misery.

Send me the rainbow of your forgiveness
and let me walk through its shimmering archway
into the clear blue day of your love.

At the Table of the Lord

Lord Jesus,
Welcome us to the place you have made ready.
Wash us clean from the dust of the journey.
Bless us as we gather as family
to eat at your table.

All God's people

Dear God,
We thank you for the people
we know today
who help us
to follow Jesus.

We thank you for the people
from days gone by
whose stories help us
to follow Jesus.

We thank you for their wise words
and their good deeds
and ask you to help us
to follow Jesus.

Let us remember before God all those
   who have died:
whose bodies now belong to
   the good earth;
whose souls are safe in
   God's eternal love
as we also are safe in
   God's eternal love.

Our Father

"When you pray," said Jesus, "say these words:

"Our Father,
who art in heaven,
hallowed be thy name;
thy kingdom come;
thy will be done on earth
as it is in heaven.

"Give us this day our daily bread
and forgive us our trespasses
as we forgive those
who trespass against us;
and lead us not into temptation,
but deliver us from evil."

Jesus said:

"If you forgive others the wrongs they have done to you, your Father in heaven will also forgive you."

Matthew 6:14

At this table

Jesus' body,
Broken bread,
By God's word
We all are fed.

Jesus' lifeblood,
Wine that's spilt,
As one temple
We are built.

At this table
Take your place:
Feast upon
God's love and grace.

A world made new

Lord Jesus, who died upon the cross:
You know this world's suffering,
You know this world's sorrowing,
You know this world's dying.

In your name, Lord Jesus, who rose again:
I will work for this world's healing,
I will work for this world's rejoicing,
I will work for this world's living.

The tree of thorns
is dressed in white
for resurrection day;
and joy springs from
the underworld
now death is put away.

The Right Path

Dear God,
Help me to find the right way to go,
even though the gate to it be narrow,
and the path difficult to walk.

Based on Matthew 7:13

Wisdom

O God,
Your word is a lamp to guide me
and a light for my path.

Psalm 119:105

O Lord,
I have heard your laws.

May I worship you.
May I worship you alone.
May all I say and do show respect for your holy name.
May I honour the weekly day of rest.
May I show respect for my parents.
May I reject violence so that I never take a life.
May I learn to be loyal in friendship and so learn to be
   faithful in marriage.
May I not steal what belongs to others.
May I not tell lies to destroy another person's reputation.
May I not be envious of what others have, but may I
   learn to be content with the good things you give me.

Based on the Ten Commandments, Exodus 20

Self-Control

God be in the little things
of all I do today
so at the end the whole may be
perfect in every way.

Spirit of God, put love in my life.
Spirit of God, put joy in my life.
Spirit of God, put peace in my life.

Spirit of God, make me patient.
Spirit of God, make me kind.
Spirit of God, make me good.

Spirit of God, give me faithfulness.
Spirit of God, give me humility.
Spirit of God, give me self-control.

From Galatians 5:22–23

Justice

O God,
We are all strangers in this world
and we are all travelling to your country.

So may we not treat anyone as a foreigner or an outsider,
but simply as a fellow human being
made in your image.

Dear God,
Help me not to speak evil of anyone, but to be peaceful
and friendly, and always to show a gentle attitude towards
everyone.

From Titus 3:2

Dear God,
Help me to be kind to someone who feels left out;
everyone needs at least one friend.

Victoria Tebbs

Courage

Trust in the Lord and do good.
The Lord loves what is right
and does not abandon those who are faithful.
He protects them for ever.
He will bless them.

From Psalm 37:3, 27–28

With my head and with my heart,
with my left arm and my right,
I will serve God through the day,
I will trust him through the night.

I sing a song of praise to God
throughout the darkest night,
for guarding me, for guiding me
to know what's good and right.
No evil things will frighten me,
no shadows from the tomb,
for God is light and life and power
to scatter midnight's gloom.

Based on Psalm 16:7–11

Faith, Hope, Love

I have faith in God above
and his everlasting love.

I have hope for heaven's shore
and God's love for evermore.

Faith and hope will pass away;
God's great love will always stay.

Faith

My faith is like a tiny seed
upon the earth below.
But heaven's blessings fall like rain
and cause that seed to grow.

Dear God, you are my shepherd,
You give me all I need,
You take me where the grass grows green
And I can safely feed.

You take me where the water
Is quiet and cool and clear;
And there I rest and know I'm safe
For you are always near.

Based on Psalm 23

I have faith in God
and I believe that I will not have to wait for heaven
to know God's goodness.

From Psalm 27

Hope

The wind from the south means sunshine,
The cloud in the west means rain,
A world in need of salvation
means Christ is coming again.

Based on Luke 12:54–56

Dear God,
When everything is going wrong I sometimes wonder
why you let bad things happen.

But then you open my eyes to the majesty of your
world, and I know once more that you are far greater
than I can imagine, and I believe once more that your
love and goodness will not be overcome.

Based on the book of Job

Love

Love is giving, not taking,
mending, not breaking,
trusting, believing,
never deceiving,
patiently bearing
and faithfully sharing
each joy, every sorrow,
today and tomorrow.

Anonymous

Help me, Lord, to show your love.

Help me to be patient and kind, not jealous or conceited or proud. May I never be ill-mannered, selfish, or irritable; may I be quick to forgive and forget.

May I not gloat over wrongdoing, but rather be glad about things that are good and true.

May I never give up loving: may my faith and hope and patience never come to an end.

Based on 1 Corinthians 13:4–7

Blessings

O God,
be to me
like the evergreen tree
and shelter me in your shade,
and bless me again
like the warm gentle rain
that gives life to all you have made.

Based on Hosea 14:4–8

Every day

Dear God, bless those who visit us: family, friends, and strangers. May we make our home a place of love and kindness for all. May we share the things we have with generosity and cheerfulness.

Victoria Tebbs

Bless me, Lord,
through my life's journey
to the place
where you are found.
Lead me safe
to your bright heaven
as I tread
this holy ground.

Night-time

Angel of God,
my guardian dear
to whom God's love commits me here,
ever this day
be at my side
to light and guard,
to rule and guide.

Traditional

Now I lay me down to sleep,
I pray thee, Lord, thy child to keep;
Thy love to guard me through the night
And wake me in the morning light.

Traditional

Father, Son, and Holy Spirit

Let the Spirit come
like the winds that blow:
take away my doubts;
help my faith to grow.

Let the Spirit come
like a flame of gold:
warm my soul within;
make me strong and bold.

Bless me, Loving Father,
Bless me, God's own Son,
Bless me, Holy Spirit:
God in three, yet one.